KARINA GARCIA'S

DIY

Slime

SIZZLE
PRESS

Hey, girl, hey!
This book is for all my fans who have been with me on this incredible journey.
–K.G.

SIZZLE PRESS

An imprint of Bonnier Publishing USA
251 Park Avenue South, New York, NY 10010
Copyright © 2017 by Karina Garcia
Text by Wendy Wax
All rights reserved, including the right of reproduction in whole or in part in any form.
SIZZLE PRESS is a trademark of Bonnier Publishing USA, and associated colophon is a trademark of Bonnier Publishing USA.
Elmer's Glue-All is a registered trademark of Elmer's Products, Inc.
Johnson's is a registered trademark of Johnson & Johnson Services, Inc.
ORBEEZ is a trademark of the Maya Group, Inc.
ARM & HAMMER is a registered trademark of Church & Dwight Co., Inc.
Bubble Wrap is a trademark of Sealed Air Corporation
Starburst is a registered trademark of Wm. Wrigley Jr. Company
CHEETOS is a trademark and brand of Frito-Lay North America, Inc.
Manufactured in the United States of America   VEP 0917
First Edition
10 9 8 7 6 5
Library of Congress Cataloging-in-Publication Data is available upon request.
ISBN 978-1-4998-0660-1
sizzlepressbooks.com
bonnierpublishingusa.com

KARINA GARCIA'S =DIY= Slime

slime

noun | \\'slīm\\

1. soft moist earth or clay; especially: viscous mud

2. a viscous, glutinous, or gelatinous substance: such as

   a: a mucous or mucoid secretion of various animals (as slugs and catfishes)

   b: a product of wet crushing consisting of ore ground so fine as to pass a 200-

   mesh screen

Per *Merriam-Webster's Collegiate® Dictionary, Eleventh Edition*

MAIN INGREDIENTS OF BASIC SLIME

- PVA (polyvinyl acetate) glue
- baking soda*
- contact lens solution*

*Most typical recipes for slime contain borax, but due to consumer concerns, Karina substitutes baking soda and contact lens solution for borax in her methods.

TABLE OF CONTENTS

PREFACE

When I started making videos in February 2015, I never thought I'd be a YouTuber. My twin sister, Mayra, had a YouTube channel, and everyone told me I should have one, too.

"You're funny," my friends said. "You have potential. You'd be GREAT!" Perhaps I was, but at the time, I was also nervous—too nervous to be filmed.

It wasn't until later that I realized I'd been making DIYs before I even knew what they were. About a year before I started making videos, I was creating makeup organizers, but I didn't have the courage to be filmed while I made them.

Eventually, I got so excited over some lipstick I made from scratch, that I grew brave.

On February 9, 2015, the day after my twenty-first birthday, I filmed myself making lipstick. Two days later on February 11, 2015, I uploaded the video to YouTube. The positive feedback I got inspired me to keep going. I'd no idea how easy it would be to create do-it-yourself videos.

Soon I started thinking about slime. At the time, there were only a few recipes for it on YouTube, but nothing particularly unusual. It was then that I began to envision ways to do something new and different with slime . . . slime with different colors, scents, textures, and recipe ingredients. Having always loved science, I couldn't wait to experiment with it! Today, 90% of my YouTube channel contains videos of slime.

At this point, I have made so many videos of slime that I've lost count! Most people assume that my home is filled with different types of slime, but the funny thing is, I don't keep any around. I film the videos in my bedroom with my younger siblings as my audience. Afterward, they scoop up the finished slime in food containers, and either take it to school to give to their friends, or keep it for themselves. My little sister has a full-blown collection that's constantly growing.

Videos of slime are my favorite videos to make because they're quick and satisfying. I also find that making slime is a stress reliever; it calms me and helps me unwind.

When I first started making videos, some people judged me because I was in my twenties and playing with slime. I found nothing wrong with it because I was doing what I loved. And now, slime has become a huge hit. It's the #1 requested video idea on YouTube. I've been told many times that people like to watch my videos one after the other! I feel lucky and grateful to be doing what I'm doing and am glad others are beginning to understand why I'm head over heels in love with slime.

This is what I've learned from my amazing experience: If you have a passion, go for it! You have absolutely nothing to lose and it doesn't matter what anyone else thinks! Never let anyone bring you down by allowing them to define you or prevent you from doing what you love.

Here's an idea: Start your own YouTube channel. If you feel nervous or discouraged, it's all the more reason to go for it! Whenever I look at some of the negative comments I receive, I just laugh and continue to do what I'm doing.

Know that every successful person was scared at one time or another. If YOU don't go for your dreams and make them a reality, no one else will. You have so much potential that you're not even aware of, so find it and use it! Go out there and live your dream!

BASIC SLIME

Although I'm constantly coming up with new types of slime, I'll never forget the old, basic slime that got me started. Whenever I make Basic Slime, I'm always reminded of the playful, creative, and slime-filled life it has led me to.

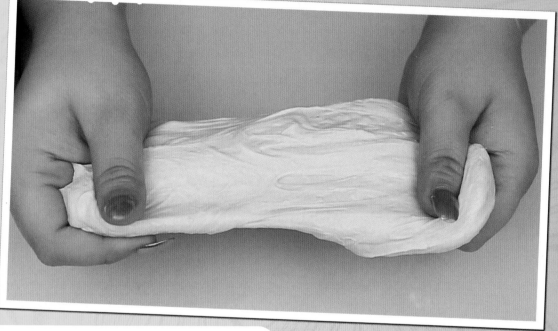

WHAT YOU NEED

- 4 oz. PVA glue

- Food coloring: optional

- ½ tsp. baking soda mixed with 3-4 tbsp. contact lens solution

- A small-to-medium-size mixing bowl

- Mixing utensil (spoon, silicone spatula, or craft sticks)

HERE'S HOW TO MAKE IT!

1 Pour 4 oz. PVA glue into the mixing bowl.

2 If you want your slime to be colorful, here's your chance! Add 3 drops of food coloring to the glue and mix it together with the utensil.

3 Slowly mix the baking soda and contact lens solution into the batter, adding only a little bit at a time— and don't use all of it. (Dumping it all in at once will ruin your batch and you will need to start over.)

4

Once the batter starts to come together into one large blob-like clump, discard the utensil and start kneading the dough with your hands. It will be a bit sticky.

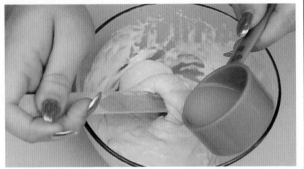

5

Add in the rest of the baking soda and contact lens solution very slowly as you continue to knead it with your hands. You'll know it's ready when it's soft and stretchy but doesn't stick to your hands.

BASIC, BUT HANDY!

Basic Slime may be simple, but it can be useful when you want to remove dirt and dust from the hard-to-reach areas of your keyboard. With its thick, goopy, and nonstick texture, Basic Slime actually makes cleaning enjoyable!

The thought of slime on my clothing made me cringe until I discovered that Basic Slime is great for removing lint. Now, whenever I spot a piece of lint on an outfit, I rip off a small piece of Basic Slime, quickly dab it on the lint, and—voilà!—the lint is gone. You can do this, too, but don't let the slime stay on your clothing too long. If you do, it can cling to your clothes and become a sticky mess. Be quick with it, and you'll be fine.

FLUBBER SOAP SLIME

This is not just *any* soap! It's squishy soap, falling somewhere between doughy and slimy. I came up with this idea by accident while attempting to make a clay-like soap.

WHAT YOU NEED

- ¾ cup and 2 tbsp. cornstarch
- ½ cup nicely scented shampoo
- 1 tsp. cooking oil or baby oil
- Food coloring: optional

- A small-to-medium-size mixing bowl
- Mixing utensil (spoon, silicone spatula, or craft sticks)

HERE'S HOW TO MAKE IT!

1 Mix ½ cup shampoo with ¾ cup cornstarch in the mixing bowl with the utensil. It will soon start to look and feel like thick paste.

2 Still mixing, add 1 tsp. oil to the batter, which will make the texture sticky.

3

Slowly pour in 2 tbsp. cornstarch with one hand as you knead the mixture with the other.

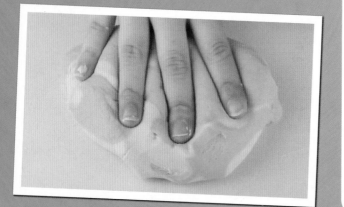

4

Optional: If you'd like to make the Flubber Soap more colorful, add food coloring! The pigment in the shampoo will have already given the slime a color, but you can switch it up with food coloring.

USE IT 'N' STORE IT!

Now, it's time to wash your hands! Tear off a pinch of Flubber Soap Slime, which is all you need, and start scrubbing away with some water. Although it is as sudsy and cleansing as regular handwash, I do not recommend using it every day because the cornstarch in it can make your hands feel dry after continuous use.

I like to keep my Flubber Soap Slime in a closed, airtight container next to the sink. It's superfun to play with, smells amazing, and is long-lasting if preserved well.

To me, Flubber Soap Slime feels like a soft, melting gum that's not sticky.

CRYSTAL CLEAR SLIME

This is one of my favorite slimes to make—especially because it looks like liquid glass!

WHAT YOU NEED

- 3 ½ oz. clear PVA glue
- 2 oz. water
- ½ tsp. baking soda
- 4–5 tsp. contact lens solution

- A small-to-medium-size mixing bowl
- Mixing utensil (spoon, silicone spatula, or craft sticks)

HERE'S HOW TO MAKE IT!

1 Pour 3 ½ oz. clear PVA glue into the mixing bowl.

2 Add 2 oz. water and mix them together with the utensil. (Water speeds up the process of making it clear.)

3 Add ½ tsp. baking soda, mixing it in.

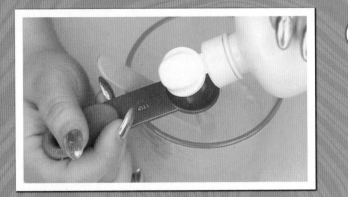

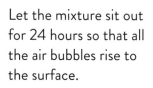

4 Add 4–5 tsp. contact lens solution, though only 1 tsp. at a time, and mix until you get a nonsticky slime. (You will have to knead it with your hands once the slime starts clumping together.)

5 Let the mixture sit out for 24 hours so that all the air bubbles rise to the surface.

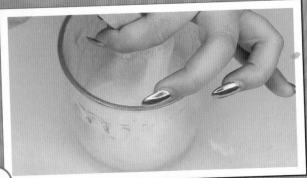

6 To make ULTRA-clear slime, remove the bubbles from the surface by simply ripping off the top layer!

WHAT I LOVE ABOUT THIS SLIME

My favorite thing about Crystal Clear Slime is its transparency, which makes it look like water! It's also fun to play with. Show your friends that you can defy gravity by holding "water" (aka slime) upside down!

BALLOON SLIME

This thick slime can be blown into bubbles! And not just your basic soap bubbles. I'm talking about giant, un-poppable, and reusable bubbles!

WHAT YOU NEED

- 4 oz. PVA glue
- Food coloring: optional
- 1 tsp. baking soda mixed with 5 tbsp. contact lens solution

- 1 drinking straw
- A small-to-medium-size mixing bowl
- Mixing utensil (spoon, silicone spatula, or craft sticks)

HERE'S HOW TO MAKE IT!

1 Pour 4 oz. PVA glue into the mixing bowl.

2 If you'd like the slime bubbles to be colorful, add 3 drops of food coloring to the glue and mix with the utensil.

3 Slowly add baking soda and contact lens solution and mix. (This is more than is needed for most recipes because it's needed to create an extra-thick slime that breaks apart rather than a runny slime that doesn't.)

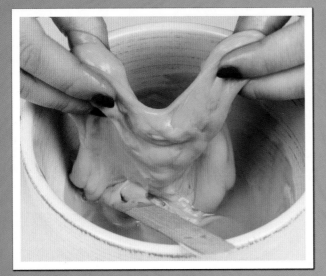

4 Once your slime starts to clump together, knead it with your hands. While doing this, continue to slowly add the remaining baking soda and contact lens solution.

5 When the slime becomes thick, test it out! Rip it apart to see if it's ready. If it doesn't rip easily, you'll need to add more baking soda and contact lens solution—a little bit at a time as you knead! You'll know it's ready when the texture is thick, stretchy, and easy to rip apart.

POP GOES THE WEASEL!

Stick the straw into your batch of slime and blow! The more slime you use, the bigger the bubbles—some may be bigger than your head! If you prefer small bubbles, rip off a small piece and blow into it. Changing the amount of slime is key to your bubble variety.

Whether it's spring, summer, fall, or winter, Balloon Slime is a blast to play with—especially with friends.

Are frozen winter bubbles a possibility?

EXPERIMENT AND SEE!

ORBEEZ SLIME

Combine two of the squishiest things together to make one of my favorite inventions: Orbeez Slime.

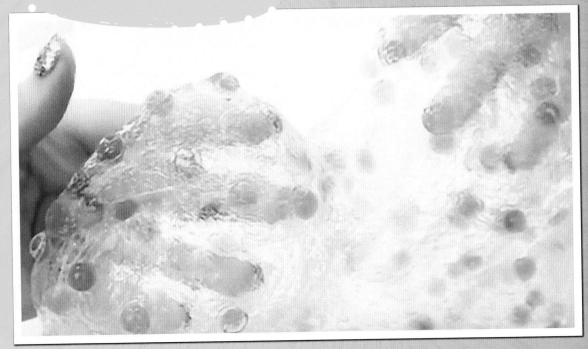

WHAT YOU NEED

- ½ tsp. Orbeez-brand polymer beads or water beads*

- 1 cup and 2 oz. water

- 3 ½ oz. clear PVA glue

- ½ tsp. baking soda

- 4-5 tsp. contact lens solution

- A small-to-medium-size mixing bowl

- Mixing utensil (spoon, silicone spatula, or craft sticks)

* These are small polymer beads that soak up water and become squishy, jelly-like beads. They're sold at craft stores and online.

HERE'S HOW TO MAKE IT!

1 Soak ½ tsp. polymer beads in 1 cup of water for 30 minutes.

2 Pour 3 ½ oz. clear PVA glue into the mixing bowl.

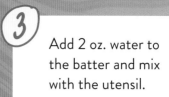

3 Add 2 oz. water to the batter and mix with the utensil.

4 Add ½ tsp. baking soda and continue to mix.

5 Add 4–5 tsp. contact lens solution—only 1 tsp. at a time—and mix until it clumps together into a blob.

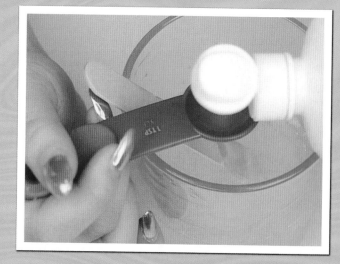

6 Knead the slime with your hands until it is no longer sticky.

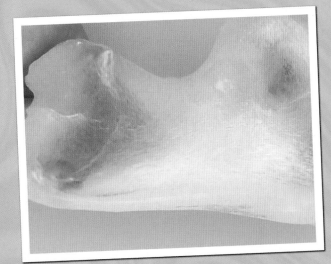

Once the slime no longer sticks to your hands, add polymer beads and knead them into the slime.

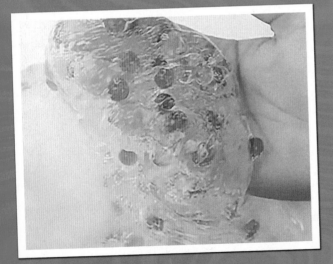

8

Put the slime in a sealed container and let it sit out for 24 hours. Afterward, you'll have super-clear Orbeez Slime.

JUST LIKE ART!

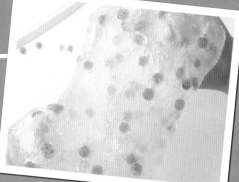

The combination of clear slime and Orbeez-brand polymer beads is one of my favorites! It makes for great décor on a desk, dresser, or shelf. You can also flatten out your slime, rip off a piece, and knead it into a masterpiece. Let it dry for 3 days, hang it on your wall, and you'll have your own customized wall art! Keep your Orbeez Slime in a clear glass jar, just so you can gaze at what looks like colorful, floating water beads.

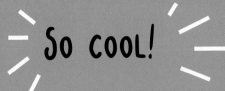

So cool!

CRYSTAL JELLY SLIME

If you've never seen a slime that appears to be filled with crystals, it's about time you did!

WHAT YOU NEED

- 4 oz. PVA glitter glue
- 4 oz. water (for glue)
- ½ tsp. baking soda
- 4–5 tsp. contact lens solution
- 5 cups water (for diaper)

- 1 non-cloth diaper
- 1 pair of scissors
- A medium-to-large-size mixing bowl
- Mixing utensil (spoon, silicone spatula, or craft sticks)

HERE'S HOW TO MAKE IT!

PART 1: The Slime Part

1 Squeeze 4 oz. PVA glitter glue into the mixing bowl.

2 Add 4 oz. water to the batter and mix with the utensil.

3 Add ½ tsp. baking soda and mix it in.

4 Mix in 1 tsp. contact lens solution at a time, using no more than 4–5 tsp. in total. Mix until the batter is not sticky.

5 Knead with your hands to bring the slime to a stretchy, nonsticky consistency.

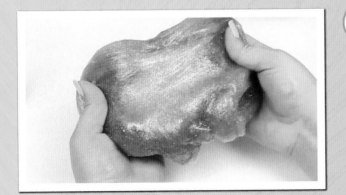

6 You'll know the slime is ready when it's squishy and stretchy and doesn't stick easily to your hands.

PART 2: Diaper Time

1 Pour 5 cups water into the diaper. This will fill it to its maximum capacity.

2 Use your scissors to cut the diaper open. The incision should be made on the inner portion of the diaper, revealing water-filled polymer crystals.

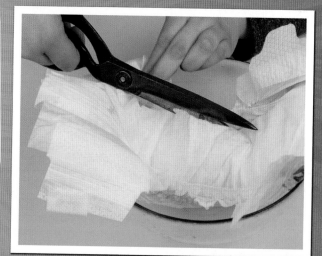

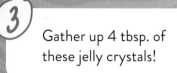

3 Gather up 4 tbsp. of these jelly crystals!

4 Add jelly crystals to the batch and knead them in!

PARTY TIME, PARTY SLIME!

Glitter glue + crystal geode lookalikes =

slime so sparkly and shimmery, you're going to

want to show it off to your friends.

HEY! WHY NOT HAVE A PARTY WITH SLIME?

LIQUID GOLD SLIME

It's gleaming . . . it's mesmerizing . . . it's Liquid Gold Slime! I am so head over heels about this royal slime, I just have to share it with you!

WHAT YOU NEED

- 3 ½ oz. clear PVA glue

- 2 tbsp. metallic gold acrylic paint

- ½ tsp. baking soda

- 4–5 tsp. contact lens solution

- A small-to-medium-size mixing bowl

- Mixing utensil (spoon, silicone spatula, or craft sticks)

HERE'S HOW TO MAKE IT!

1 Squeeze 3 ½ oz. clear PVA glue into the mixing bowl.

2 Add 2 tbsp. metallic gold paint and mix with the utensil into the batter.

3 Add ½ tsp. baking soda into the batter and mix until the baking soda dissolves.

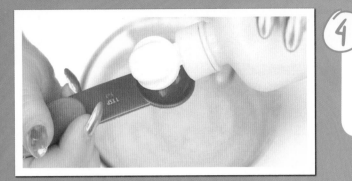

4 Mix in 1 tsp. contact lens solution at a time, using no more than 4–5 tsp. in total.

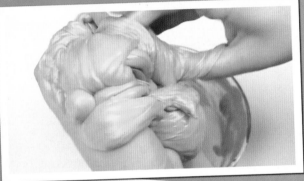

5 Discard the utensil and knead the slime with your hands until you have a nonstick consistency.

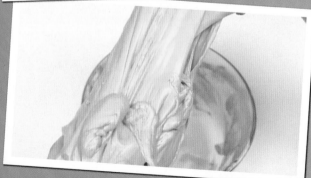

TAKE IT FURTHER!

You may just want to bask in the sparkle of this
hunk of slimy gold, but if you're still in creative mode,
here's something fun to do:

1. Shape your slime into cool, flat shapes and let them
   air-dry for 3 days.
2. Once they're dry and solid, add some craft
   glue to the back.

YOU'LL HAVE AWESOME, CUSTOMIZED, GOLD 3-D STICKERS TO SHARE WITH YOUR FRIENDS!

BUBBLE WRAP SLIME

Like Bubble Wrap, Bubble Wrap Slime is sure to turn everyone—including the oldest, most mature person in the room—into a kid again. How can anyone resist the chance to POP, POP, POP?

WHAT YOU NEED

- 4 oz. clear PVA glue

- 3 oz. water

- ½ tsp. baking soda

- 4–5 tsp. contact lens solution

- 1 cup transparent fish bowl filler beads*

- A small-to-medium-size mixing bowl

- Mixing utensil (spoon, silicone spatula, or craft sticks)

* These are small, round, flat beads made of hard plastic found at most craft and décor stores. They can be any shape, but remember not to get the jelly ones.

HERE'S HOW TO MAKE IT!

1 Pour 4 oz. clear PVA glue into the mixing bowl.

2 Add 3 oz. water to the batter and mix with the utensil.

3 Add ½ tsp. baking soda and mix until it dissolves.

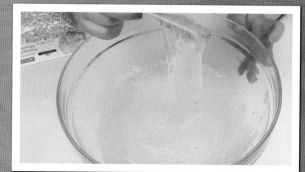

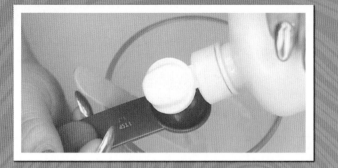

4 Mix in 1 tsp. contact lens solution at a time, using no more than 4–5 tsp. in total.

5 Discard the utensil and knead the slime with your hands. Once it's thick and stretchy, it's ready. It's okay if it's a bit sticky, it'll make it easier for the beads to stick.

6 Knead 1 cup filler beads into the slime. The more beads you have, the less sticky your slime will be.

TWIST, SQUEEZE, POP!

Twist and squeeze your Bubble Wrap Slime to enjoy the POP, POP, POPPING! Here a pop, there a pop, everywhere a POP, POP, POP! You may drive some people crazy . . . or you may inspire them to make some Bubble Wrap Slime of their own.

FRUITY, CHEWY SLIME

Here's a slime* that's not just stretchy. It's tasty, too! Yes, you can eat Fruity, Chewy Slime! You can choose your favorite flavor or create a mix of them.

WHAT YOU NEED

- 6 cups water
- ½ cup unwrapped Starburst candies
- 1 cup powdered sugar
- 1 tsp. cooking oil
- A small-to-medium-size pot

- 1 small glass stovetop-safe container
- Stovetop
- 1 silicone spatula
- Oven mitts (adult supervision is required with these)
- 14-inch piece of baking parchment paper

* Please note that this recipe is a bit more complicated than the others in this book, and you'll need an adult to help you.

HERE'S HOW TO MAKE IT!

1 Pour water into the pot until the water level is 2 inches deep.

2 Pour ½ cup unwrapped Starbursts into the stovetop-safe container.

3 Place the stovetop-safe container with the Starbursts into the pot of water, and put the pot on the stovetop.*

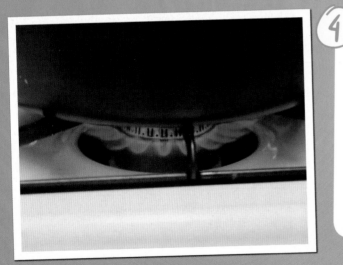

4 Turn on the burner beneath the pot to medium-low heat, and DO NOT LEAVE IT UNATTENDED. Slowly stir the Starburst mixture, and it should melt within a few minutes.

* This is known as the double-boiler method.

5 When the mixture is fully melted, turn off the burner, and let it sit for 2 minutes. It will cool just a little, so DON'T TOUCH IT! It will be hot, hot, HOT!

6 Using oven mitts, remove the stovetop-safe container with the Starburst mixture from pot.

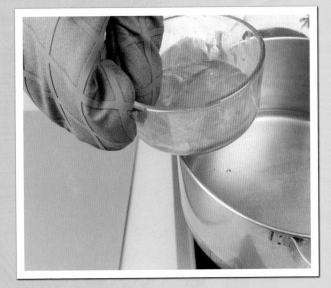

7 On a nearby surface, lay out the 14-inch sheet of parchment paper. Sprinkle only ½ cup powdered sugar on its surface. (This will keep the mixture from sticking to your table or countertop.)

8 Grease your spatula with cooking oil.

9 Using the spatula, pour the melted Starburst mixture onto the parchment paper. Though it will be super-sticky, the oil on the spatula will help it slide off.

10 Let the mixture cool down for 3 minutes. After that, check it every minute with the spatula. If it stretches too easily like goop, it is still too hot and needs to cool for another 2 minutes or so. When you stick the spatula in and the mixture feels thick and stiff, you'll know that it's ready.

11

Slowly add your remaining ½ cup powdered sugar to the batter as you fold it in with the spatula. If it becomes too stiff, go back to the double-boiler method (step 3) for 1 minute and it will soften right up! Then let it cool down again for 1–3 minutes.

12

Once you've added the sugar and the mixture has cooled down, it's time to use your hands! Start kneading until your Fruity, Chewy Slime is no longer sticking to your hands!

THE FUN'S NOT OVER YET!

Now, you have a choice: Do you play with your slime, or do you eat it? I say do both! Fruity, Chewy Slime will go over really well at birthday parties. You can let everyone choose their own Starburst flavor (or gummy bears, Gummy Life Savers, or other gummy candy, if preferred). I came up with this slime after being unsatisfied with the taste of other edible slime. My goal was to make my slime sweet, yummy, and fun to play with. Now, I know how to do it—and so do you!

GLOW-IN-THE-DARK SLIME

Here's a fun way to turn a boring slime into something super-cool!

WHAT YOU NEED

- 4 oz. clear PVA glue
- 1 tsp. glow-in-the-dark powder*
- ½ tsp. baking soda
- 4-5 tsp. contact lens solution

- A small-to-medium-size mixing bowl
- Mixing utensil (spoon, silicone spatula, or craft sticks)

* I have only found this online. Do not use glow sticks, which may contain toxic elements!

HERE'S HOW TO MAKE IT!

1 Add 4 oz. clear PVA glue to the mixing bowl.

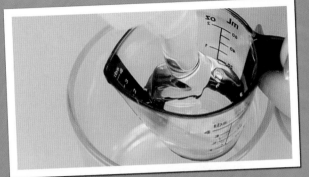

2 Add 1 tsp. glow-in-the-dark powder to your batter and mix with the utensil.

3 Add ½ tsp. baking soda and mix until the baking soda dissolves.

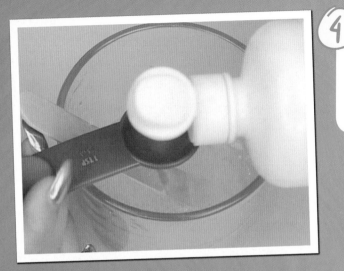

4 Mix in 1 tsp. contact lens solution at a time, using no more than 4–5 tsp. in total.

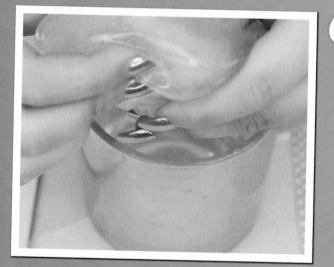

5 Once the slime has formed into a blob, starting kneading it with your hands. The slime will be ready when the stickiness disappears.

HERE'S HOW TO USE IT!

Turn off the lights to get the full effect of your awesome Glow-in-the-Dark Slime! This slime is fun to use at a sleepover, on Halloween, and at any other "lights out" get-together. Put some of this slime in a clear container and you'll have a homemade night-light!

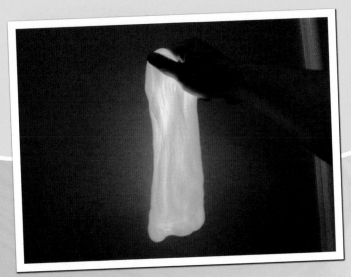

FLUFFY SLIME

Imagine a big, fluffy cloud in your living room—made out of slime! This must-try Fluffy Slime recipe is one of my all-time favorites. It's light, dense, and fun to play with.

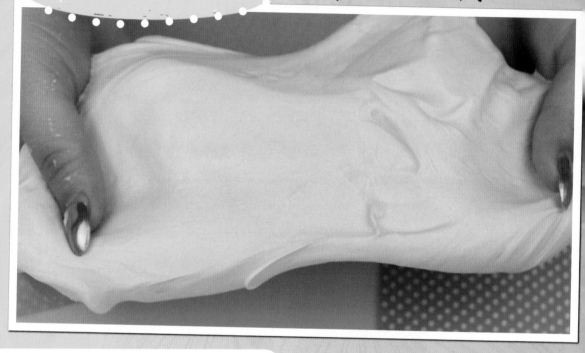

WHAT YOU NEED

- 4 oz. PVA glue
- 1 ½ cup shaving cream
- Food coloring: optional
- 8 tsp. contact lens solution
- A small-to-medium-size mixing bowl
- Mixing utensil (spoon, silicone spatula, or craft sticks)

HERE'S HOW TO MAKE IT!

1 Pour 4 oz. PVA glue into the mixing bowl.

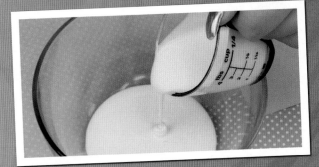

2 Add 1 ½ cup shaving cream to the batter and mix with the utensil.

3 Optional: Add 8 drops of food coloring. (This is more than most recipes require and is needed to compensate for the shaving cream, which tends to mask color.)

4 Slowly drizzle 1 tsp. contact lens solution into the bowl as you mix. Continue to do this with the remaining 7 tsp. (If you add the contact solution too quickly, you run the risk of ruining the slime, which means you'll have to start over.)

5 Knead the slime with your hands. You'll know it's ready when the slime feels manageable in your hands without sticking to your skin!

TIME CHANGES SLIME!

How do you change Fluffy Slime into Iceberg Slime? Let it sit out uncovered for 3 days. This will cause the top layer to harden. Press down on the slime and the surface will start to crack—just like an iceberg!

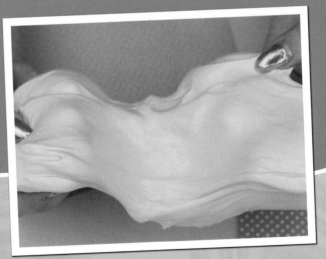

KARINA'S BRAND-NEW SLIMES!

COFFEE SLIME

Whether you're a coffee drinker or not, this slime smells just like coffee . . . which is super-delicious. Inhaling its wonderful scent relaxes me. I just have to remember NOT to drink it!

WHAT YOU NEED

- 1 oz. water

- 1 tbsp. instant coffee

- 4 oz. PVA glue

- 1 tsp. baking soda mixed with 5 tbsp. contact lens solution

- A small-to-medium-size mixing bowl

- Mixing utensil (spoon, silicone spatula, or craft sticks)

- 1 coffee cup/mug (optional)

HERE'S HOW TO MAKE IT!

1 Mix 1 oz. water and 1 tbsp. instant coffee in the mixing bowl with the utensil.

2 Add 4 oz. PVA glue to the batter.

③

Slowly start adding baking soda and contact lens solution to the mix. (If you add it all at once, it will not work and you'll have to start over.)

④

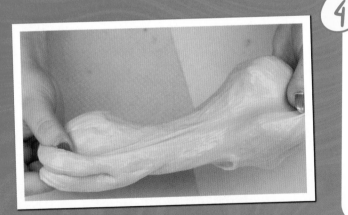

Once all the baking soda and contact lens solution has been added, start kneading the mixture with your hands. When it's no longer sticky, your Coffee Slime will be ready!

THIS SLIME WAS MADE FOR SMELLING— NOT EATING!

As yummy as Coffee Slime smells, it is not edible or drinkable. So if you put it in a mug to trick your friends, make sure they don't try to take that first "delicious" sip, or any other sips. It's the smell that makes THIS slime great.

NONSTICK ULTRA-THICK SLIME

If you don't like sticky things, this mess-free recipe is for you. It may look like chewed-up gum, but it's missing the stickiness and shine.

WHAT YOU NEED

- 4 oz. PVA glue

- Food coloring: optional

- ¼ cup baby powder

- ½ cup shaving cream

- 1 tbsp. hand lotion

- 1 tsp. baking soda mixed with 5 tbsp. contact lens solution

- A medium-size mixing bowl

- Mixing utensil (spoon, silicone spatula, or craft sticks)

- An uncovered container

HERE'S HOW TO MAKE IT!

1 Add 4 oz. PVA glue to the mixing bowl.

2 Optional: If you'd like color, add 8 drops of food coloring to the batter and mix with the utensil.

3 Add ¼ cup baby powder to the mix and stir until it becomes fluffy.

4 Add ½ cup shaving cream to the batter.

5 Add 1 tbsp. hand lotion and stir it all together. This will make the slime stretchy.

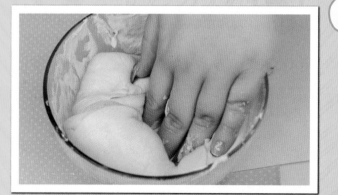

6 Slowly pour baking soda and contact lens solution into the mix until the slime is not sticky. Then knead it with your hands to thicken the consistency.

7

The slime should be thick, but not as thick as it needs to be. Let it sit uncovered in a container for 24 hours.

8

After a complete day, your Nonstick Ultra-Thick Slime will feel like putty. The top will be stiffer than the rest, but if you knead it, it will soften.

WHO KNEW?!

This nonstick slime is so thick, it has a similar consistency to rubber. Yes, it can even bounce! So feel free to roll it into a ball and bounce away!

HOT 'N' CHEESY SLIME

As a big fan of Flamin' Hot Cheetos, coming up with a recipe for Hot'N'Cheesy Slime is one of the coolest things I've ever done—even though this recipe is not edible!

WHAT YOU NEED

- 4 oz. clear PVA glue

- ½ tsp. red acrylic paint

- ½ tsp. baking soda

- 3 tsp. contact lens solution

- 1 cup Flamin' Hot Cheetos

- 1 resealable plastic bag (any size)

- A small-to-medium-size mixing bowl

- Mixing utensil (spoon, silicone spatula, or craft sticks)

HERE'S HOW TO MAKE IT!

1 Add 4 oz. clear PVA glue to the mixing bowl.

2 Stir ½ tsp. red acrylic paint into the batter with the utensil.

3 Stir ½ tsp. baking soda into the mix.

4 Add 3 tsp. contact lens solution—1 tsp. at a time—to the mix until you have sticky slime.

5 Put 1 cup Flamin' Hot Cheetos into a resealable plastic bag, close it, and crush them with your hands into little pieces.

6 Pour the Flamin' Hot Cheetos bits from the bag into the slime, and knead them into it with your hands.

MAKE YOUR OWN CHIP SLIME!

Your Hot 'N' Cheesy Slime will smell so good,
I must remind you again not to eat it. It's fun to play
with though, especially since the oils in the Flamin' Hot
Cheetos make the slime supersoft and stretchy.
Hot 'N' Cheesy Slime makes a great gift, as do other
slimes that you can make by using other types of chips in
the recipe above. A great way to preserve your
Flamin' Hot Cheetos—or "Other Chips"—
slime is in an empty candle container.

KINETIC DOUGH SLIME

This slime is truly unique! Kinetic Dough Slime stretches like slime but molds like Kinetic sand, which is a sand that mimics the physical properties of wet sand and is used for sculpting and indoor play.

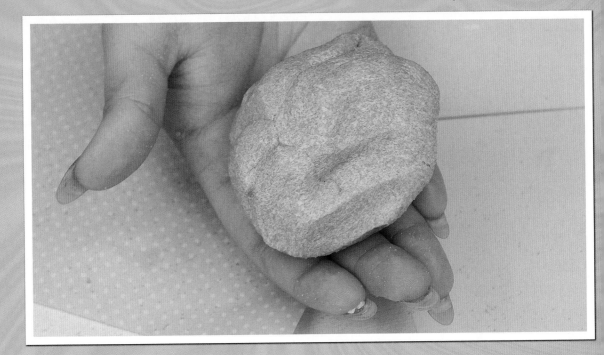

WHAT YOU NEED

- 2 oz. PVA glue

- Food coloring: optional

- 5 tbsp. sand*

- ½ tsp. baking soda mixed with 2-3 tbsp. contact lens solution

- A small-to-medium-size mixing bowl

- Mixing utensil (spoon, silicone spatula, or craft sticks)

* You can buy sand at any craft store, or you can use real sand from the beach or outdoors.

HERE'S HOW TO MAKE IT!

1 Pour 2 oz. PVA glue into the mixing bowl.

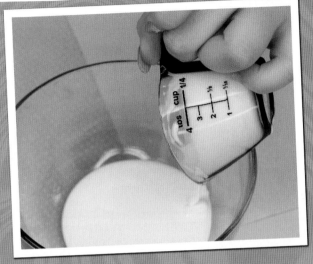

2 Optional: Stir in 3 drops of food coloring with the utensil to give color to the slime.

3 Add 5 tbsp. sand—1 tbsp. at a time—to the batter and mix. Once the sand is added, you should have a super-thick, sandy glue.

4 Slowly start adding baking soda and contact lens solution. (You may not need the whole thing.)

5 Once the slime has formed into a blob, stop adding baking soda and contact lens solution and start kneading it with your hands. The slime will be ready when the stickiness disappears and it feels like nonstick dough.

LIFE'S A BEACH!

Next time you go to the beach, bring home some sand and create your own one-of-a-kind Kinetic Dough Slime!

DID YOU KNOW?

FUN FACTS ABOUT KARINA

- I was born in Orange, in Orange County, which is part of Los Angeles, California.

- I have a twin sister named Mayra who also has a YouTube channel. She does beauty videos and her channel is mayratouchofglam.

- I have three brothers and two sisters.

- In early 2015, I lived in a three-bedroom mobile home with my parents and all five siblings! Imagine all eight of us living in a three-bedroom home! In September 2015, I moved into an apartment with my twin sister, and in April 2016, I leased a house for my parents, four of my siblings, and me. More recently, I was able to buy a house on one property with two more properties attached for my whole family to share. That's not the only way my online business has changed our lives. It has also allowed my parents to retire! I now pay them a monthly allowance and they don't have to pay rent or bills. My dad sure doesn't miss working long hours in construction!

- I was super-shy as a child—to the point that I'd start crying whenever I found myself in any awkward situation. My shyness stayed with me until I was like twelve.

- My boyfriend has been my cameraman for all my videos from the beginning.

- My first video of slime was Flubber Soap, which I made when I was twenty-one. I uploaded it on August 12, 2015.

- It takes me at least two days to put one video together. I spend about two hours planning, four hours filming, six hours editing, and a couple hours making thumbnails!

- I've had at least five videos that didn't work out and were never uploaded.

- I attend many YouTube events. After most of them, I go back to my hotel room and cry—not because I'm sad, but because I'm happy and grateful to have so many amazing supporters.

- Contrary to what people think, I don't have a collection of slime at home. What I make, I give away, and whenever I feel like playing with slime, I just whip up a new batch. I also give away other DIYs of mine, such as liquid pens.

- My birthday is February 8.

- Subscribers often say they're nervous to meet me. The funny thing is, I'm usually just as nervous to meet them. (Maybe even more so!)

- I started out filming all my videos in my old bedroom, which was a mess! Not just a mess—a full-blown disaster! The only clean part was the bit that showed up on camera. However, in my new house, I now have my own filming room.

- I'm wearing pajama pants in most of my videos. I figure that since viewers can only see my top half, I might as well be comfy!

HEY, GIRL, HEY!

MAKE SURE TO **FOLLOW ME** TO KEEP UP WITH EVERYTHING GOING ON IN MY WORLD!

YouTube: /TheKarinaBear

Instagram: @karinagarc1a